SO YOU WANT

TO WRITE!

I0161961

Basics of writing, publishing & marketing

R. Frederick Riddle

TABLE OF CONTENTS

From the Author

This eBook has been written with you the author in mind. You may have come across some of the ideas expressed here in other venues. However, in putting this book together I have tried to impart specific guidelines plus Tips, Examples, and Applications.

The structure will appear as follows:

Principle

    The underlying principle being taught.

Tips

    Author's tip(s) related to subject.

Example

    An example of principle in action.

Application

    Applying the principle to overall strategy.

Instead of an in-depth manual, this book is a series of brief articles covering some of the most important aspects of being an author. The Author's Basic Writing Template is based on this book and is a useful tool in itself.

You may have received the Author's Basic Writing Guide when you got this book. The guide is geared to this book and is designed to give you the fingertip experience. In other words, many ideas and tips from the book are included in the guide. Use it either as an aid in using the book or as a stand-a-lone guide.

Return to Top

Why Do You Want to be a Writer?

Why?

That is a key question in life. And that is just as true for today's writer as any other life activity. Which brings us to our first principle.

Principle

Discover WHY you want to write.

Sounds simple, but knowing why you want to write is virtually as important as knowing how to write. It requires soul searching.

The Why may change over time and therefore you should always keep track of it. Not only the change itself but the reason for the change.

Tips

1. ***Ask yourself why you want to write?*** What are your motives, and expectations.
2. Take your time. Better yet, take a sheet of paper and start writing down reasons for writing. Don't reject anything at this time. Lay it aside for a day, then review it, crossing off

those that don't really measure up. *Keep doing it until you have your primary motive.*

3. Motivation is the backbone of your writing. When you hit the wall or get discouraged or encounter difficulty, you will return to your motive.

4. *Christian authors should have another motive: The Call of God!* If He called you to write, then that is a supreme motive.

*E*xample

What excites your literary inner you?

When I ask myself those questions I come up with several answers:

- o It's God's plan for me.
- o The simple joy of writing.
- o The satisfaction of seeing my story in print.
- o The desire to convey an idea or thought to others.
- o The chance to make money.
- o Fame.

*A*pplication

Any person wanting to accomplish anything needs a plan. Even God had a plan when He created the world. Authors also need a plan.

One of the things that I have learned over the course of my writing career is to have a flexible plan. A plan that can be adjusted to reflect new knowledge and/or ideas.

That plan begins with knowing why you want to write. That is why I made a list. I put God first in the list because He planned for me to write before I was ever born. All other items flowed from that fact.

But success as a writer requires a plan, which you will see unfold in this book.

Return to Top

What About Genre?

First, we need to explain Genre. It is defined in Wikipedia as: *A literary genre is a category of literary composition. Genres may be determined by literary technique, tone, content, or even (as in the case of fiction) length. The distinctions between genres and categories are flexible and loosely defined, often with subgroups.*

*P*rinciple

There are many Genre subgroups. So you, the author, must decide where your writing fits.

Discovering your genre will be a valuable aid not only in marketing, but in the writing and publishing of your book.

Don't brush this aside. When I first began writing I didn't even know what genre was, let alone which one I was under. At best I knew that I was writing fiction.

As time went on I began understanding the meaning and importance of genre. The more I learned, the better my writing and my marketing.

*T*ips

1. Take a close look at your writing. It is probably more than a single genre. And that is good!

2. ***Identify all the genres your book would fit within.***

*E*xample

In my case I write both fiction and non-fiction. In the fiction arena my genres have been American History, and Bible history. But my writing genres are also: Adventure, Romance, and even some Mystery.

My non-fiction works have been on American History, Bible History, Politics, and How To.

*A*pplication

Identifying your genres will be crucial when you get around to marketing your books. It will also help you in determining such things as your audience.

As stated in the Principle it also affects your writing and publishing. In writing, knowing your genre keeps you on mark. Meanwhile in publishing, it helps you in selecting your publisher.

Return to Top

Work Place

*P*rinciple

If you have already been writing for awhile you know how important your workspace needs to be for optimal results. This includes the table/desk, the chair, location of resources, and more. So let's take a look.

The Room

The location and size of the room will vary from author to author. My wife prefers an open room, while I have a small, well-defined room. Both of us have our desks in front of a window. Teresa's files are in different cabinets not necessarily adjoining each other, while I used a combination of cabinets and bookshelves to create the "walls" of my room.

Both of us like our setups and are able to function well. This is important. Whatever setup you choose, it needs to be conducive to your being able to think, research, and write. My suggestion is for you to design it your way even if others may criticize. You are the one who will be spending a lot of time there!

One other note, sometimes Teresa likes to move into the living room and sit at the table. This gives her a break from the norm while still enabling her to perform her tasks.

The Table/Desk

Once again personal preferences are dominate. Teresa uses a computer desk while I use a computer table. She tends to spread paperwork out, I like things a little tighter.

But once again our own wants and needs strongly influence how it is done. As for how the table/desk is set up, both of us use laptops on the surface. I have a phone beside me, she doesn't (except when in the living room).

Never place your laptop on your lap. This is because you may be blocking air vents. Buy yourself a lap desk (there are several).

The Chair

Both of us prefer task chairs, but I have seen others who use Executive Chairs. The key here is that you want a chair that is comfortable, but also helps you maintain good posture. This last is important because slouching in your chair cuts off oxygen and causes you to get sleepy. It is very hard to write with your eyes closed!

Another note regarding sitting with a laptop on your lap even with a lap desk. There are issues with back strain, eye strain, etc. that are affected by sitting with a laptop.

Location of Resources

As mentioned before I use my cabinets and bookshelves as the "walls" of my office. This keeps everything close by, easy to reach. Teresa has her resources spread out, but that seems to work for her.

The important thing is that it be helpful to your overall work.

The Resources

What do I mean by resources? Well, this covers:
- books on writing
- books on the Bible (necessary if writing Biblical books)
- books on marketing
- financial records
- publishing information

- o Research material
- o and more

Your resources will differ from ours, but you will have a need for them and you will need to keep them somewhere safe and easily accessible.

You need to also consider such factors as lighting, storage (paper, ink, incoming/outgoing, and more).

*T*ips

Your workspace is exceeding important. ***Take time to make sure it meets your needs!***

*E*xample

It is not uncommon for me to require some research. By having resources close by I am able easily make use of several resources, including my computer.

As mentioned I use a task chair as it is both comfortable and work friendly. By using that plus a computer table I am able to sit for long periods of time and accomplish whatever work needs to get done.

*A*pplication

When planning your work space you need to take time to analyze your needs. It may require the investment of money as well as time. Remember that you need to know what your needs are because an uncomfortable or inefficient work space will make it very difficult for you to be an effective writer.

Return to Top

Your Audience

This can be a bit tricky. Especially for new authors. If you have previously written books then you already have something to gauge who your audience is.

Principle

So there are three principles:

1. **New Authors:** Make use of reviewers. Who are they, especially those with a positive view.

2. **Established Authors:** Review your sales data to see who buys your books, and who reviews your books.

3. **All Authors:** Look at other authors in your genre. Who is in their audience?

In summary, the principle is to make use of reviews, sales, and audiences of other authors.

Tips

Make a list of audience possibilities. ***Then narrow the list down*** until you have gotten it as refined as possible.

Example

When I first began writing, I thought my audience would be men. After all I am a man and I was writing historical fiction which included adventure. But actual sales tipped in the direction of women. While I now market to both sexes, I see women as my primary audience, although I now write for both.

*A*pplication

Don't check out your audience and then forget it. Periodically check it out again. Then apply that knowledge to your marketing, but don't forget the actual writing and publishing.

Return to Top

Plotting Your Story

*P*rinciple

I look at plot as the framework of the story. In other words, the structure upon which you build your story and insert characters, scenes and the like.

The plot is essential. Without it your story will ramble, bore, and ultimately fail. The plot does not guarantee success of the story, but no plot will guarantee the story will flop.

*T*ips

Whenever writing your book always keep the plot in mind. ***Every scene should somehow connect with that plot.*** The plot is the necessary framework and you are the engineer building the story character by character, and scene by scene.

*E*xample

In my novel *Dead Eye Will* the plot was basically the story of a young man who fought in the War of 1812 and later became an agent for the Governor of the Michigan Territory. That plot spanned many years from 1813 until 1836 as William Riddle earned the reputation of Dead Eye during the war and later.

It chronicles his growth as a mere boy into manhood, his service both in the army and civilian life. That is another aspect of plot: it chronicles events.

*A*pplication

You probably have a library filled with books in your favorite genre. Examine some of them and you will see how important plot is to the story. As with other aspects of writing you can find entire books written on the subject of plotting. Check out your library or your local bookstore and you will find some excellent books. But mostly **remember to keep your plot in mind when writing.**

Return to Top

Know Your Character

Characters are the second most important part of your story. How well you structure them and how well they fit with the plot can determine the success or failure of your story.

But the principle that I want to zoom in on is knowing your character.

I am sure you are aware that many articles have been written about building characters in a story. The following idea is a method I use and, hopefully, different than what you have previously heard or read.

To begin with most advice is to create a list of your hero's or anti-hero's characteristics: height, weight, color of eyes, hair style and color plus habits, likes, and dislikes. This is all good and helpful, but why not take it further?

When I write I become the character I am writing about. Not just the primary character, but to some extent every character. For example, in my book *Perished: The World That Was* there were several dominant characters, including Adam, Cain, Enoch, Methuselah, and Noah just to name a few. In addition there were various supporting characters.

Here is what I do: *I become the character.*

For example, when Adam was talking or doing something, I became him. I saw what Adam saw, experienced what he experienced, and thereby made decisions. These decisions were his not mine the author. How did I do that?

First, although Adam is an historical person, I am the person who created his personality in the book. Second, because of that I knew him and felt him. And third, I let my imagination impose his personality upon mine. Finally, Adam became the author, writing his scenes.

Does that make sense?

Chances are you have gone through a similar process but just didn't realize it. You know your character inside/out, so why not take that next step and let the character take control?

And not just your main character. Extend this to every character that has some kind of role. Obviously your main character will dominate, but the other characters also come alive.

If you have never tried this before, it can be scary. But I encourage you to try it, to experiment with just one character. I think you'll like the result.

*T*ips

Use your imagination. You either created the character, created the character's personality, or at least recorded the character's characteristics. Let your imagination focus on the character, become that character, and let the character speak through you.

It's not easy at first, but once you have done this I think you will see its value. The truth is that you already do this as a reader; you become the character you are reading about. As a writer, you allow the reader part of you do the same thing but as an author.

*E*xample

In my book *Perished: The World That Was* Adam and Eve have sinned and been expelled out of the Garden. They are driven out through the only entrance and can never get back in.

In the ensuing scene they are outside the Garden and must walk down a long natural ramp to the ground below (in the story the Garden is raised above the surrounding area at least a hundred feet).

As they make their way down the ramp Adam's love for Eve overcomes him. Although he originally blamed her for his sin, he realizes it was his fault not hers. He stops and comforts her.

To write that scene I had to imagine I was Adam and Eve my wife. And the question arose: How am I going to comfort her?

By allowing Adam to have control the scene pretty much wrote itself.

*A*pplication

This technique is primarily for the main character, but you can use it for other characters as well. The trick there is to keep your characters separate and not confuse one for another. This takes you back to that list of their characteristics.

Return to Top

Location of Story

Principle

> Where (and when) does your story take place? This is not as critical to your story as you may think. Stories have been written (see Example) where the location is never disclosed to the reader without hindering the story itself.

> However, if you do state a location, whether fact or fiction, you want to be sure of your description. This is especially true of actual places. You don't want a reader who has been there to dispute your facts.

Tips

> When identifying a location that is a real place be careful with your description. ***It must be as factual as you can make it. Even fictional places need to be believable.***

Example

> A good example of this was a story (don't remember the name) where a man owned two cats who helped him solve mysteries. The thing is you never know the city or even the region he lived in other than the Midwest.

*A*pplication

Putting this principle to work requires a bit of research on your part. If you are writing about a place you have never been then it is imperative that you do research.

You will want maps, geographical descriptions, economic analysis of the area, and much more. I would say that you can't get too much information.

This is true even when writing historical books. When writing *Perished: The World That Was* I had to research the first five hundred years after the Flood. Why? Because little is known outside the Bible's narrative of what that world was like. By looking at the rise of civilization after the Flood I got a peak into the past.

Even writing futuristic novels taking place in outer space requires research. For instance, you want to be correct in describing the galaxy and known stars.

So be careful.

Return to Top

Resources

*P*rinciple

Once upon a time an author had few resources he/she could use to help their writing careers. Today that is not true.

I am only going to deal with aids in writing, but the truth is there are plenty of reliable resources that you can use for publishing and for marketing.

Make use of the resources available to you whether books or internet.

Here is a brief list of what is available:

- o books on writing
- o books on the Bible (necessary if writing Biblical books)
- o Research material
- o and more

*T*ips

1. **There is no excuse for not having information.** We live in the age of the

internet. You can search for just about anything. But be careful. The internet is rife with false and misleading information. While it can be a rich source of material, you have to be careful.

2. Another Tip is to **bookmark your favorite resources**. Chances are you will need them in the future.

*E*xample

For my Bible related stories I make use of books on the customs and manners of the people, historical references, and names of men and women in the Bible. In addition, I make use of commentaries of the related person or event, word studies, and more.

But I don't restrict myself to books. We live in the age of the internet. So I make use of it, searching for all manner of information. This requires a discerning spirit as there is false as well as true information on the internet.

*A*pplication

When I am researching something on the internet I use the search function a lot. Sometimes I don't have a book on the particular subject or I want further information. In either case, I search for the needed information.

As you know a whole list of websites come up. I look through them. If I find a site that I have found reliable in the past I will look there. That doesn't guarantee anything, but it is an important step.

I will stop at different sites and evaluate their content. Sometimes I know enough about the subject to see how accurate the site is, but sometimes the information is entirely new.

In this case I may evaluate the site itself. Who controls the site? Is it recommended by others? In other words, can I trust it?

Build your library with books, ebooks, and well bookmarked resources.

Return to Top

Page Setup

Principle

Page setup is critical to your book. Different publishers have differing requirements, but I will show you two possible setups.

1. Standard 11 x 8.5

    Top: 1"

    Bottom: 1"

    Left: 1"

    Right: 1"

    Gutter: Usually the same as Left (if publisher asks for a gutter)

    Although this is considered standard, the book is reduced by the publisher to a smaller size such as 9 x 6.

2. eBook 9 x 6

    Top: .79"

    Bottom: .79"

    Left: .79"

    Right: .79"

    Gutter: none

    (A printed 9 x x6 book's gutter would be same as Left.)

Some publishers require Headers/Footers, while others don't want them. So you need to find out what your publisher wants. Which means that you may have to go back and copy the manuscript with a unique name and redo the margins, headers, etc.

*T*ips

If possible, do your setup before you start writing. We use the 9 x 6 setup. *But whatever you use, set it up first, you can always change it later.*

*E*xample

This book's setup includes the 9 x 6 eBook margins. Since it is an eBook and not in print there are no page numbers, headers, or footers.

*A*pplication

We use the 9 x 6 setup because we are in charge of our publishing. If we use an outside publisher and they have different standards we can make an additional copy just for them.

Return to Top

Starting Scenes

Scenes are like the pieces of a crossword puzzle. Individually they may be interesting but when placed in the proper place that they form an integral part of the puzzle.

Each scene, in a sense, is a miniature story. While by itself it can't stand, it does have something to contribute. Basically each scene should have four parts: Plot, Character, Theme, and Suspense.

How long should a scene be?

The answer to this is in the context. For example, Plot, technical information, and scenic descriptions should all be short scenes. On the other hand, conversation, emotion, and suspense often require longer scenes. Don't over think it. If you are a reader as well as a writer you will likely know which works best.

There are many ways to start a scene. Books have been written on crafting and you should build a library on writing. But a good start is to consider using these techniques:

1. begin with action
2. begin with conversation
3. begin in the middle
4. begin with a promise or anticipation
5. begin with a problem
6. begin with the setting itself
7. begin with the time of day

These are just seven techniques.

*T*ips

1. **Before and after writing a scene consider the four parts (Plot, Character, Theme, and Suspense).** Is the reader reacting the way you planned?
2. **You should feel when you have it right**.
3. **No matter how you write your scenes you need to clearly separate them.** I use the ampersand (&), some use (xxx), and others use other markers. But don't use blanks!

*E*xample

&&&

Adam awoke. *Something caused me to wake up. What was it? Wait - Eden River. That is it! I must have been dreaming about Eden River.*

Gently disengaging himself from Woman, he got up. Being as quiet as possible, he headed for the river where he found a comfortable knoll. From this position, he had a good view of the river. *It must be about a half-mile across! I never realized that. Tomorrow, I will take Woman and we will follow the river to its beginning.*

In silence, he continued watching the river, estimating its size. The question was its length. A glitter caught his eye. He smiled as he realized that the moon's light seemed to dance on the river's surface.

After awhile, he returned to Woman where he lay down and was soon fast asleep.

&&&

This scene taken from *Perished: The World That Was* takes place in the Garden of Eden. Notice that it is brief (scenes can vary in length), it relates to the Plot, concerns Adam, and sets up the reader for the next event (exploring the river).

Did you notice how scene started? "Adam awoke." While not the most exciting beginning it does denote sudden action. It attracts the reader's attention with an implied 'something is about to happen.' In other words, it opened with action, although mild.

The sooner you get to action in your scene the better. But beware that the action is appropriate to your character(s).

And I used separators before and after!

Application

When writing a scene you want this mini-story to excite or intrigue or provide necessary information to your readers. In the example above the scene prepared the reader for Adam and Eve's exploration of the Eden River plus it gave information about the river itself.

When you break your story up into scenes it becomes easier to edit, move, or even delete scenes as deemed necessary.

Return to Top

Middle Scenes

*P*rinciple

The middle of your scene is primarily where the bulk of the story occurs. The opening of the scene prepared the reader for what was about to occur and now it is happening.

While it is true that the middle of the scene usually falls into the middle of the scene (duh), sometimes writers actually begin their scene in the middle. And that is an important thing to remember.

Don't be stuck in your approach to scenes; experiment with moving the parts around. See what works best. Sometimes opening with the middle works.

That said, it is usually best to have the middle actually take place in the middle. Let the opening set it up.

It is in the middle of the scene where you will see and, hopefully, feel the character's response to the opening. What is the character going to do in response? Is their further action?

A middle scene is usually the bulk of the scene's story. It is also usually the longest. **It is where the response to the opening unfolds.**

*E*xample

&&&

Adam awoke. *Something caused me to wake up. What was it? Wait - Eden River. That is it! I must have been dreaming about Eden River.*

Gently disengaging himself from Woman, he got up. Being as quiet as possible, he headed for the river where he found a comfortable knoll. From this position, he had a good view of the river. *It must be about a half-mile across! I never realized that. Tomorrow, I will take Woman and we will follow the river to its beginning.*

In silence, he continued watching the river, estimating its size. The question was its length. A glitter caught his eye. He smiled as he realized that the moon's light seemed to dance on the river's surface.

After awhile, he returned to Woman where he lay down and was soon fast asleep.

&&&

This is the same example I used for showing the opening of the scene. This time I want you to take note of the middle. Notice that beginning at "Gently disengaging" and ending at "on the river's surface" Adam is responding to his dream and goes to observe the river. During this time he views the river, mulls over the river's width, and makes plans for the future. All this in a short scene.

*A*pplication

You shouldn't put to much thought into this in your first draft. Write your story (say, chapter) then go back and examine individual scenes.

Keep in mind that each scene plays an integral part in your story and the middle is very important.

Return to Top

Ending Scenes

*P*rinciple

The ending scene either draws the scene to a conclusion or sets the reader up for the next scene. Sometimes, when having multiple subplots, you need the scene to at least temporarily draw to a close because in the next scene you will be viewing a different subplot.

Ending Scenes, therefore, are very important and should not be approached carelessly. Unless you are creating suspense or something akin to it, the reader should not be left dangling aimlessly. At the same time you want the reader's anticipation to be alive. This is a fine line, but I would err on the side of mystery.

In some respects it is because of the anticipation factor that the Ending Scene is so critical. So spend some time thinking about it. Does the scene draw to a satisfying close? Do you, as the reader, want to continue reading? Is there anything that can be done to improve the scene?

Whether you are closing a scene or pointing to the next scene you want your reader desiring more.

*E*xample

&&&

Adam awoke. *Something caused me to wake up. What was it? Wait - Eden River. That is it! I must have been dreaming about Eden River.*

Gently disengaging himself from Woman, he got up. Being as quiet as possible, he headed for the river where he found a comfortable knoll. From this position, he had a good view of the river. *It must be about a half-mile across! I never realized that. Tomorrow, I will take Woman and we will follow the river to its beginning.*

In silence, he continued watching the river, estimating its size. The question was its length. A glitter caught his eye. He smiled as he realized that the moon's light seemed to dance on the river's surface.

After awhile, he returned to Woman where he lay down and was soon fast asleep.

&&&

You will notice that I have again used the same example. There's actually a plan here. While it is not the perfect scene it embodies all three aspects of good scene writing: Opening, Middle, and Ending.

The ending is actually very short: 'After awhile, he returned to Woman where he lay down and was soon fast asleep.'

In this case the scene was drawn to a close. The body or middle had already pointed to the next scene so that would have been redundant.

Please note once again that the scene started and ended with a separator, in this case the '&&&.' The separator is extremely important. (I had one book where the publisher removed the separators and left only line feeds. That was terrible!)

*A*pplication

As mentioned in the Middle Scene application you should keep in mind that each scene plays an integral part in your story and, in this case, the ending is very important. The reader should be experiencing whatever emotion you want him or her to feel.

Scenes, and I am speaking of all three aspects (Opening, Middle, and Ending) play a crucial role in your story. In effect, this is where "page turning" occurs. The reader's desire for more action, feeling, or whatever is being satisfied yet not completely fulfilled. You want them wanting more.

Don't let that scare you, though. As mentioned previously, when writing your first draft don't focus on your scenes. Let the story spontaneously write itself if possible. Then go back and edit.

It is in these edits that you concern yourself with your scenes. And Don't fall in love with a scene. If it isn't working, you will need to change it or delete it. Or even move it.

Return to Top

Watch Your Grammar

*P*rinciple

Your grammar must be perfect!

Right?

Depends on who you talk to and the specifics involved. Here is my take:

Generally speaking you want your grammar usage as correct as possible, but there are exceptions. For example, let's say one of your characters only has a ninth grade education.

You would not want that character talking like a professor. For that matter, you really don't want any of your characters to talk that way unless they actually are professors.

Now I don't recommend that you try to imitate slang and accents, but just be cautious. Maybe allow a character to have a favorite saying. In *Perished: The World That Was* I had Methuselah with a favorite saying, "So God has said, so shall it be."

Which brings up a related principle: Be consistent. If I later had someone else using that same phrase it could have been a jolt. Be consistent.

So here's the principle: When you are dealing with conversation (or even thoughts) you can and should be less than perfect but consistent. Everything else should be perfect.

Aside from speaking, there is the matter of punctuation and spelling. With the tools available this should never be a problem, but it does occur. It is therefore necessary to check your spelling and punctuation as often as possible.

*T*ips

Be consistent. If Bob is talking like a country boy on page 2 and a professor on page 132, you better have shown a transformation. ***Your reader will spot inconsistencies!***

*E*xample

The boys is clothed alike. This is poor grammar.
The boys are clothed alike. Much better.
"You guys look the same." OK.
"The boys is clothed alike," Martha said. OK, if this is consistent with Martha's education.

*A*pplication

Both my wife and I try to watch our grammar usage. One of the tools we use is Microsoft Word's grammar checker. It's not perfect, but it helps. Also, we use the spell check, but it is not always up-to-date.

Other resources are grammar books (especially older versions that really emphasized good grammar), and the internet.

Make use of as many resources as needed. And pay attention to grammar and punctuation when editing.

Return to Top

Knowing Your Viewpoint (1st, or 3rd)

*P*rinciple

Viewpoint or Point of View is critical to your story. The Point of View allows the reader to experience someone else's view of the world.

Before looking at the viewpoints let me give you another related principle: Make sure your reader knows when the character is thinking and when he is speaking. And try to avoid he thought or she thought.

We are going to take a look at two POV (Point of View). These are 1st Person and 3rd Person.

First Person

This is essentially "I", "Me", "Mine". The POV is from the speaker. He/She tells the story from His/Her perspective. Personally, I don't like this POV but I have read some excellent books using that technique.

There are a few advantages to this viewpoint, such as:

- o Instant involvement

  Because the reader is inside the character's head all thoughts and actions are immediately known. There is no delay.

- o Language

  Because the reader is inside the head and knows the thoughts of the character the reader is able to instantly know the education, and class of the character.

- o Range

  How the character thinks. The reader learns a great deal about the character because every facet of his/her thinking is open to the reader.

But there are also disadvantages; such as:

- o it requires the presence of the character in *all* scenes.
- o the character can't keep secrets from the reader. If the character knows something, we do also.

- you cannot include any information that the character doesn't know. In other words, you know what the character knows. No more and no less.
- The "I" becomes both you and the character. This can be troubling.
- limited view. Since you only know what the character knows there is a whole world of unknowns.

First Person, in my opinion, is harder to write and to pull off. Some authors do and succeed quite well. But it can be unwieldy. Therefore, unless you have a great deal of experience in writing, I would recommend you stay away from it.

Third Person

Third Person, in my opinion, is the preferred method to use. It is the "he", "she" or "it" viewpoint.

The advantages of this POV are:

- an outside view of the person
  You, the narrator, can talk about other facts, events and people.

- you can have additional characters in third person

  you can have other POV characters.
- unlimited worldview
- In the first person you were restricted by the author's or character's thoughts and opinions.
- But in third person the narrator and reader have access to other information - thus expanding the scene.
- greater objectivity - in first person you only have the character's opinion of self, but in third Person you see much more and can make better judgments.
- hidden information - In third person the author can keep some facts about the character secret until later in the story.

But there are disadvantages. These include:
- separated involvement

  With first person you had instant involvement, but here there exists separation or distance between the character and the reader.
- language

  It is more difficult to identify the class and education of the character.
- range

Awkward. The thinking, etc, is not as visible as it is with first person.

*T*ips

1. **Choose your POV carefully**. First person identifies more closely with the character, while third person more distant. Also, third person is better, perhaps necessary, when dealing with multiple characters.
2. **When conveying a character's thoughts put it in italics**. Not a hard rule, but I recommend it.

*E*xample

First Person: I thought to myself, What a wonderful day!

Third Person: He looked about, smiling. *What a wonderful day!*

*A*pplication

Be careful with your POV. It is very easy to forget which POV you are using. The result can be disastrous.

I do not recommend First Person, although many authors have done so successfully. It takes a lot of hard work and skill. And in my opinion is too limiting.

Be aware also that there are many variations of both first person and third person viewpoints. I recommend that you buy a good reference book on the subject. There are many resources, including Writers Digest.

That said, I practice something a little different: Multiple Third Person. It is the most difficult of all to master. But if you do, it is worth it.

See my article on Multiple Third Person.

Return to Top

Multiple Third Person Viewpoint

*P*rinciple

Imagine yourself as a reader who gets to read the minds of the characters. Not necessarily all the times, but at critical times. It gives you, the reader, the power and knowledge to understand what is going on to a greater degree.

In Third Person Viewpoints you are reading or "listening" to the thoughts of the primary character. But in Multiple Third Person Viewpoints this is multiplied so that the reader has the opportunity to grasp more and understand more.

That being said, I would not suggest too many characters at one time. Generally I try to limit to two or three characters. And only with the primary character do I have constant contact.

*T*ips

1. **Generally, multiple characters with observable viewpoints should be introduced early**. However, in books spanning many years it is possible to distant them (as in Perished: The World That Was).

2. Unless you are truly great with **prose keep your primary character as your primary POV**. In books like Perished you can change the primary character but make sure the transition is smooth. You must transition between POV's. You will lose the reader if you don't.

*E*xample

In *Perished: The World That Was* you have a book covering 1656 years. It starts with Adam being the primary character but he eventually dies and another takes his place. This continues until Noah becomes the primary.

In each case there was a transition (either death or simply a "changing of the guard" (so to speak)).

I do not recommend doing this in a story that is more compressed in time. Most likely your primary character will be constant throughout.

Another example from the same book is the inclusion of multiple primary characters. But it is rare for both to appear in the same scene at the same time. If such a situation presents itself, however, only one should be the primary at that time.

*A*pplication

Multiple Person Viewpoint is in my opinion the most flexible (and hardest) viewpoint for the author to use. That flexibility is a valuable asset for the author. so don't shy away from it.

Try it out. Buy books on viewpoint and learn what works for you.

Return to Top

Scheduling

*P*rinciple

Really! Everyone knows how to schedule don't they?

Unfortunately the answer is no. Not because the people are stupid. They were probably never taught to schedule.

I learned the hard way of the necessity to schedule my time. As I entered the multifaceted world of writing, publishing, and marketing I found my time to be precious. Everything and everyone wanted it.

One of the best books on the subject I ever read was Success God's Way by Charles Stanley. He had a whole chapter devoted to time. It is based on Ephesians 5:15-16: "See then that ye walk circumspectly, not as fools, but as wise, Redeeming the time, because the days are evil."

However you do it, it is necessary that you schedule your personal and professional time.

But Scheduling is more than use of time, it is making priorities. Every day I make a short priority list - by short I mean no more than three items.

This is not your typical "to-do" list, but it is related. Think of it this way, make your "to-do" list and select the top two or three.

If you are like me, having a long list usually leaves items undone and me a little discouraged. But when I limit it to two or three there is a much better opportunity for me to accomplish all of them!

Scheduling also involves appointments. As an author you will need to keep track of when you are to meet with or contact agents or publishers or even reporters, when you are supposed to do a book signing, and many other events.

Tips

1. Redeem the time: **make good use of your time. Schedule it.**
2. **Make your "to-do" list and select the top two or three.**
3. **Do it!**

*E*xample

I actually schedule my time beginning with my morning devotions. I have what I call Focus. I usually focus on two, sometimes three items related to writing. I also write them down in my calendar.

However you do it, make it a habit. You will quickly discover just how valuable a habit it is!

*A*pplication

Scheduling is not really rocket science, but it does require thought. It rests firmly on your concept of what is truly important for your writing career. It is one of your most important priorities.

So if you have never put down a to-do list before do it now. It's easy. Start by writing down, in no particular order, every thing you think is important to be done.

Then narrow the list down to seven or ten items (still no order).

Now you have what I call a typical to-do list. Your next step is very difficult: arranging the items in order of importance. I suggest three categories: important, more important, and most important.

That will probably take some time, but your next step requires you to take the top three. By this time everything should be in order of priority. But it is possible that the top two or three items may be tied. If so, you need to narrow it down further.

To help you get to your final two or three items, ask yourself what needs to be done and what has to be done.

Now you have your list of two or three must do items. The final step is the most important: **Do it!**

Return to Top

First Draft

PC Readers

Let me take a moment and introduce you to the concept of PC Readers. First there is PCE or Proof Copy Editing. I use this term because typically writers are confusing editing with proofing. (To learn more go to PC Editing).

Proofreading is typically a separate activity of examining the final draft to make it ready for publication, but copyediting involves a more thorough examination. There you check grammar, spelling, word use, and consistency.

Since this book looks at you as an independent author-publisher-writer it accepts the notion that you will be assuming many responsibilities of a publisher.

The term PC Reader is not a professional reader, although they could be. The duties include reviewing the book chapter by chapter. I recommend having several PC Readers, each using a different colored marker.

PC Readers should like to read, be able to read at a high school level or above, be able to follow directions, and be trustworthy.

You can draw your readers from your friends and family. And they should be rewarded! This does not mean financial rewards, but rather something like acknowledgment in the front of your book, a free copy of the book, or a gift certificate. And yes, if you want to, you can reward with money.

Now let's look at the First Draft.

*P*rinciple

There are many approaches to this subject. But before discussing let me give some terms.

First Draft: Refers to the completed yet unedited manuscript. It is also known as the rough draft.

Second Draft: The resulting manuscript after the original or first draft has been copyedited. Upon finishing this draft you would employ PC Readers.

Third Draft: This is potentially your final draft.

So a Second Draft is the novel as it exists after the first edit by you but before you employ the use of PC Readers. If you are like me you really don't want someone else reviewing your work in its unedited form. The First Draft therefore is the result of your unhindered writing. While you may have edited along the way your story is in its roughest form.

It is at this time that you perform your first edit. At this juncture you do not use a PC Reader. This edit is primarily by you (although your spouse or best friend could act as an extra pair of eyes).

Here's an optional idea: If your first PC Reader is trusted (spouse or friend) you might want that person to review your work. You would then edit it.

FIRST DRAFT

I encourage you to edit as you write. Some authors prefer not to do this, but I find it an excellent way to keep the story on track. More importantly, it allows you to take productive breaks; that is, a break away from the writing of the novel while you perform basic editing.

BASIC EDITING

There is no hard and fast rule for this method. I suggest that at the completion of each chapter you stop, review the chapter you just finished and correct any errors you discover.

Generally, you look for common errors like spelling, grammar, and voice consistency. This is not an intense review. By that I mean that when I do this I am simply doing a casual read of the chapter and making corrections as they pop up.

If you follow this practice your First Draft will not be as rough as it might have been. It is not hard nor time consuming and usually results in a stronger First Draft. And you are ready for the Second Draft.

The main principle here is to proof and edit your first draft to eliminate errors and other undesirable things found in the manuscript. Then repeat until it is as perfect as possible.

In this article I won't be discussing Professional editors other than they can be very valuable if you can afford them.

But if you are doing it by yourself (a dangerous prospect) you need to involve others. Seems like a contradiction, but that simply means that you make use of friends and other non-professionals. While even this has its drawbacks, it will help raise the quality of your work.

(Professional editors are not perfect either.)

So how do you review and edit your work?

I have a very simple method that has been honed over a number of books. Here are the steps:

1. Review the manuscript
2. edit the manuscript
3. have another party (usually my wife) review it
4. I edit it again
5. have another party (friend, acquaintance, etc.) review it
6. edit it again
7. repeat #5 & #6 until satisfied

Like I said, it is a very simple method but you have to start somewhere. Don't get me wrong, you can always benefit from a professional. But if you do hire one *make sure that you have the final say.*

Tips

Review and edit your first draft to eliminate errors and other undesirable things found in the manuscript. Then repeat until it is as perfect as possible.

When using friends or others to review your book reward them (it doesn't have to be monetary).

Example

The method listed below is simple but effective. Feel free to steal it and modify it.

1. Review the manuscript
2. edit the manuscript
3. have another party (usually my wife) review it
4. I edit it again
5. have another party (friend, acquaintance, etc.) review it
6. edit it again
7. repeat #5 & #6 until satisfied

*A*pplication

An important thing to remember is that there is no perfect book. Period!

I am sure that there are writers who will argue with that statement but the burden of proof lies with them. I have read classics and found errors.

Face it, there will be errors. But your job is to make that as impossible as you can. So follow the plan I showed or make a better one. When you are finally sure it is perfect it is ready to be published.

Return to Top

Second Draft and More

Principle

This draft is a result of your first edits. But it is unlikely that it is finished.

Why do I say that? After all, you had yourself and others read it and you edited. Surely it is ready.

It might be. But I recommend that you do at least one more edit. I usually do two or three. I read and edit, my wife reads and I edit, and I do a final read and edit.

Believe it or not we still find errors or things that need to be changed. Sometimes it actually results in rewriting scenes to better fit the story.

Tips

1. **Don't be afraid to do more edits.** Your story will be better for it.
2. **Listen to your those who have helped you in your editing.** Their ideas may prove very valuable to the final work.

3. **Consider printing one copy of a single-sided book.** Not required, but I find it helpful in the editing process.

*E*xample

I usually do two or three more edits using the method described above.

This usually results in a better manuscript. Sometimes I actually rewrite scenes because I have had the time to observe and listen to my Readers.

*A*pplication

The Second and following drafts are among your most important. Each time you are likely to improve the overall story strength and appearance.

At this time you may be getting impatient and just want to get it over with. But don't stop now. Your best work may be just ahead!

Return to Top

PC Editing

Principle

I have previously talked in general terms about your editing. But what do you really do when reading and editing.

My wife and I hit upon something that has helped us. Instead each person looking for all possible errors, we each look for something different.

For example, maybe I look for spelling, my wife looks at grammar, another looks continuity, and still another looks at something else. Then in future edits we may change who looks at what or maybe look for something else.

This does not mean that if I am looking at spelling and I spot poor grammar that I ignore it. I take note and correct it.

Tips

Each person reading take a different aspect so you are not duplicating one another.

*E*xample

In one book I read and edited, then my wife read and I edited, a third person read and I edited, and finally a fourth person read and I edited.

*A*pplication

Reading and Editing are not to be taken lightly. Take the time to apply the principles I have provided. Don't just read once and believe that you have got it

Maybe you are really confident in your abilities and you really don't believe me when I emphasize the importance of reading and editing. So you are tempted to ignore the warnings.

If you do ignore the warnings, you will most likely fail. Reviewers will score you low because of errors and poor grammar.

Why risk it? You invested a lot of yourself in the writing of the book, it and you deserve the same effort be put into the final drafts!

Return to Top

Do I Need An Agent?

*P*rinciple

When I began writing my very first novel I set out looking for an agent. I knew enough to look for those agents that operated in the same genre I was writing but not a great deal more. So realizing my shortcomings, I took to the internet.

What do agents do?

That's a fair question and there are at least three things they do:

- o Submit your manuscript to possible publishers
- o Negotiate contracts
- o Distribute money (royalties, etc.)

While all of these were appealing to me I soon discovered getting an agent wasn't all that easy. I discovered something right away.

- o Finding an agent in my own genre is time consuming
- o I needed to know what I wanted in an agent

- o Not every agent is accepting new clients
- o My book needed to pass their approval
- o Seeking a publisher can be more productive

I also discovered that some publishers require the author to have an agent and won't even look at your manuscript unless there is an agent. But more on this in another article.

It was at this time I started looking at self-publishing more seriously. It changed my life, but that will have to wait for another article.

When I decided to use a self-publisher I found I wasn't required to have an agent (although some people suggest it would help). I simply chose the publisher and submitted my manuscript. However, throughout the writing and publishing process I still thought it a good idea to have an agent. In fact, for a time I continued to look for one.

Eventually, after considerable time and effort, I found an agent I liked and submitted a query letter to her. It turned out that the particular genre I was writing wasn't in her interest area, so that fizzled. I continued looking, but didn't really find anybody else that was both available and desirable.

As a result I have never had an agent. Here are some reasons why:

- o It can take months to find the right agent
- o That agent may not want you
- o Agents are not required for self-publishers

So one of the primary reasons for getting an agent is to find a publisher for the book you have invested so much time in writing. That reason becomes nullified when you choose a self-publisher. But they are also helpful, for a fee, in marketing your book.

Could I have benefited from an agent? Probably. But being on a limited income and not being able to find the right agent (in spite of excellent resource material), I opted out. Which means that I had the added responsibilities that agents normally handle, which is quite a chore.

So what should a new author seek in an agent or should he look at all? Would you be better off with or without an agent?

Ultimately you make that call. There are many factors in choosing an agent. I do believe it would be wise to at least explore the possibility. So check out my article on Choosing An Agent.

*T*ips

Some publishers require the author to have an agent and **won't even look** **at your manuscript unless** **there is an agent.**

It is important to KNOW what you want in an **agent: Genre, experience, client testimonials,** **and fees.**

*E*xample

Agents come in all sizes and shapes. I chose not to go with an agent after being turned down by the one I wanted, after finding out most agents were either tied up with other clients or weren't accepting new clients at that time.

This was a very frustrating time, but I persevered.

*A*pplication

Please don't ignore agents simply because I chose not to have one. I actually wanted one but it didn't work out. It is possible that an agent could have spared me much anguish and disappointment.

Agents have a lot to offer. They will review your manuscript, make editorial suggestions, and generally guide you toward preparing it for prospective publishers.

So seriously look for an agent. But if you decide to opt out then please note that everything they would have done for you is now upon you. That means finding a publisher, signing a contract, as well as all the marketing responsibilities.

Return to Top

Choosing An Agent

Principle

Choosing an agent is a very important and taxing process. This article won't cover it all, but should help you have a better grasp.

First of all, you need to know that not all agents are desirable. You could become an agent today even though you may not be truly qualified. There are no tests, certificates, or any earned degree.

There are resources which I will point to that can help in determining qualified agents. You can also contact them and ask about their experience, how many clients do they have, who are their most famous clients, and if they charge a fee (red flag!)

That means that you have the burden of sorting them out, but before you do that you need to know WHAT you are looking for in an agent.

Here is a list of desirable qualities:
- o   A qualified agent (see above)
- o   Agent is interested in same genre as you

- You actually like the agent (read their blogs, talk to them)
- Visit their website & read submission guidelines

Be careful about fees. Most reputable agents charge a commission and don't charge reading fees. Reading fees should be a turn off.

There are many resources out there to check. I will mention a few but I do not personally know them. So do your research. They are listed here in alphabetical order:

- AgentQuery.com

  A database of literary agents is a free service. Has 1000 listings of agents.

- Books and Such Literary Management

  A literary agency that covers a complete range of services for authors.

- PublishersMarketplace.com

  A complete resource database. Requires a $25 monthly fee.

- pw.org (Poets & Writers) directory

  A free database on literary agents and agencies.

- o QueryTracker.com

  Free database for search agents and agencies. Has over 200 publishers and 1000 agents.

- o WritersMarket.com

  Database of 400-600 agent listings. Subscription price $5.99 per month.

*T*ips

Most reputable agents charge a commission and don't charge reading fees. Reading fees should be a turn off.

*E*xample

Poets & Writers is both a directory and a magazine resource for information on contests, writing tools, grants, and more.

*A*pplication

When researching and choosing an agent to represent you remember that traditional publishers often *require* authors to have agents. Self-publishers generally don't make such a requirement, but they will work with them. So you need to consider whether you are going with a traditional or self-publishing publisher.

If you decide to get an agent, make use of the sources mentioned in this article. There are also others that can be found on the internet. Simply search for "book agents," "literary agents," or something similar.

Return to Top

Seeking A Publisher

Principle

How does one seek a publisher? First, you must decide what kind of publisher you need. See the articles on Self-Publisher, Traditional Publishing, and You, the Publisher.

This is actually a critical decision. Unfortunately there is a lot of mudslinging going on. Not to mention confusion. In my articles on the different types of publishing I strive to clear it up a little.

But before you make that decision you will want to search the internet and discover who and what these publishers are. Even more important, is to decide the overall direction you want to go.

In future articles I examine each type of publisher closer, but here it is important that you know what *you* need.

Here are just a few things to examine:
- How long are you willing to wait for your book to be published?

- o Can you afford $400 or more upfront.
- o Are you a new author.

There are other considerations as well. But these three will give immediate indications. For example, traditional publishers often have time lines that result in books being printed as much as two years down the road after signing the contract. On the other hand, self-publishers want you to pay for the privilege which often involves $400 or more.

And if you are a new author there are some publishers who will not consider you. These are generally found in your larger traditional printing houses.

Then there are publishers who are like self-publishers but have a minimum order requirement. For instance, I knew of one author who had to buy $5000 worth of copies at a time, which required storage.

*T*ips

Examine what your needs, perceived and known, are before searching for a publisher.

*E*xample

When I wrote my first novel, I didn't know about costs, time, or submission requirements. So I began looking for a publisher while in the dark.

Fortunately, I had access to the internet and began learning fast. It didn't take me long to figure out that traditional publishing was not for me. While they are free and pay royalties, they were too restrictive.

For example, the traditional publishers often required an agent (I didn't have one) plus prospects for publishing soon were unreasonable (up to two years after signing).

I eventually signed with a self-publishing firm. It cost me about $400 upfront plus the cost of marketing tools which they sold.

*A*pplication

It is your responsibility to find the right publisher for you. Everybody has an opinion, but you are the one who has to live with your decision.

Read my articles on the different types. Weigh the facts and decide which one best works for you.

Return to Top

Handling Rejection

Principle

This is primarily addressed to those of you who plan to use a traditional publisher. Self-publishing companies rarely reject a manuscript.

As a disclaimer I have never received a rejection slip because I have never used traditional publishers.

That said, I can say this with authority: Never let rejection slips stop you!

Use them as you would any tool. Learn from them. Why was the manuscript rejected? Did it come with any suggestions as to how you can improve? If so, you should consider them (but don't violate your own standards).

Another thing to remember is that editors have their own ideas as to what makes successful writing. They are not THE authority.

Tips

Use rejection slips as learning tools to help you become a better writer. Don't take it personally.

Example

Since I have not been rejected I have no practical example to share. But the more meaningful example is one's reaction to any roadblock, which is all that a rejection slip amounts to in one's career.

That said, check out your response to other roadblocks. If your response works in those cases, maybe it will with rejection.

But better is this: *As I said in the Tips: Use rejection slips as learning tools to help you become a better writer and don't take it personally.*

Application

My suggestion is to stay away from Traditional Publishers and this is only one reason. But if you must use Traditional Publishers, then please use restraint in listening to them.

You have a responsibility to yourself. That is why I emphasize treating rejection as a tool. Instead of being discouraged, see it as something that will only make you a better writer!

Return to Top

Self-Publishing

Principle

Self-Publishing is coming into its own. It has been around for awhile now with resulting improvements in quality and acceptance.

I mentioned in a previous article that self-publishers rarely reject a manuscript. That is true, but some do reject if the manuscript is deemed of poor quality. Or they may require additional editing.

But it is still true that you rarely get rejected. If you are willing to pay the fee (usually $400-$800) they are willing to publish. That said, thorough editing should be done *before* submitting the work.

There are many self-publishers out there. What follows is an alphabetical listing of some of the better known houses:

- o AmericaStar*
- o AuthorHouse***
- o Bookbaby
- o CreateSpace

- DiggyPOD
- iUniverse***
- Lightning Source
- Lulu
- Outskirts Press
- Smashwords**
- Tate Publishing
- Trafford Publishing***
- Xlibris
- Zulon Press****

* Now known as America Star. Is actually between self-publishing and traditional. Cost is free and offers a royalty (although small).

** Publishes ebooks only. It is free.

*** Owned by Author Solutions.

**** Christian Self-Publishing.

When I started writing I made use of AuthorHouse and America Star. In both cases I was pleased with their work. In fact, any of the houses mentioned above probably provide excellent quality and service.

*T*ips

Self-Publishing has been around for awhile now with resulting improvements in quality and acceptance.

Self-Publishers rarely reject a manuscript.

There are many self-publishers out there.

*E*xample

As mentioned I have used two of the houses listed. Their cover quality was very good (very important) as was the overall print quality.

I did my own marketing. America Star provided me a little more help although AuthorHouse may have caught up since I last published with them in 2003.

*A*pplication

If you are choosing between Traditional and Self-Publishing, Self-Publishing is the better in my opinion. That said, there is a better way.

Return to Top

Traditional Publishing

Principle

Unless you are an established author it is very difficult to get with a traditional publisher. That is because the houses are well established, have a reputation, and, probably, don't want to take a risk on an unproven novice.

Even so, it is not impossible.

As mentioned in a previous article, many of these Traditional Publishing Houses will not even consider a manuscript unless the author is represented by an agent.

This is good because when dealing with them you need to have the expertise and knowledge of the agent on your side.

It is also important to remember that some traditional publishers specialize in genre. Some only want established authors. Some may temporarily suspend new acquisitions because they already have a boatload.

But there are some traditional publishers looking for new authors. If you write Christian fiction you may be interested in Christian publishers. There you will find a list of publishers that publish Christian works, including fiction.

Additionally, you can access a list of publishers at Everywritersresource. This is a list of publishers taking submissions.

If you are willing to take a chance on publishers that accept unsolicited manuscripts (and may not require an agent), try this list.

Finally, if you are looking for a traditional publisher that accepts new authors try Karen Fox.

*T*ips

Traditional Publishers are well established, have a reputation, and, probably, don't want to take a risk on an unproven novice.

There are lists of publishers taking submissions, accepting new authors, and Christian publishers.

*E*xample

Never having been published by a Traditional Publisher, I can't give you a personal example. But you can access their websites and discover their guidelines, list of clients (authors), and success stories.

*A*pplication

Traditional Publishing has a long success story. They aren't going away soon. If you feel that you have written a quality story that will sell and you are willing to wait, then traditional publishing may be for you.

Make use of the lists provided here and study them. You just might strike it rich!

But don't forget, some of these publishers will require you have an agent. So if your heart is fixed on one of the top publishing houses, get yourself an agent!

Return to Top

You, The Publisher

*P*rinciple

These days the author has more responsibility than ever before - and more opportunities!

In days gone bye the author wrote a novel, submitted it to a publisher, and once accepted, relaxed. But that is no longer true!

There are all kinds of publishers out there. But here I want to present you with a different perspective. In a previous article I mentioned that there is a better way than self-publishing. You are about to see what I was talking about.

First a brief history. I published my first novel in 2003. Since then I have written a number of books. The first four books were all published by self-publishers. But in 2013 I discovered Smashwords.com and published my first ebook. (My other books are also in ebook format but publisher did this because I paid for it.)

This discovery has changed my life and now I am about to reveal to you what I believe is a better way to publish.

That better way is simply: You are the publisher!

Although there is almost no information on the subject out there I know I am not the first to engage in this activity. Essentially it is still a form of Self-Publishing. However it is called Indie Publishing.

Indie Publishing is the author taking ultimate charge. Basically it means selecting a printer or publisher to print our books. And there are publishers out there willing to be our printer and even our marketer.

The one I am most familiar with is CreateSpace. I will discuss that more in the example. I have also located at least one other printer called Best Value Copy. They are an online printing service that provide quality work at reasonable prices.

In looking for a quality printer you can try your own neighborhood. For example, there is a Staples store not far from us that gives business discounts to authors using their printing services. That suggests the possibility that other office supply stores may offer the same services.

But assuming the role of publisher is more than just getting a printer. You literally take on the responsibilities of a publisher. You may have to seek your own ISBN, copyright, and other important items.

In our case, we listed ourselves with the State of Florida with a dba (Doing Business As) name of T&R Independent Books. Eventually we will probably need to buy ISBNs and copyrights.

It is both exciting and scary. But the rewards can be awesome. For example, a self-publisher may give us anywhere from 8% to 40% royalty depending on volume of books sold. But as our own publisher the percentage goes up to 80% and more (after costs and taxes).

In addition to that, we have virtual control over every aspect. It is true that with CreateSpace some control lies with them, but it is also true that such controls are limited.

In establishing our own publishing business we also took on the marketing of the books, which will be discussed in my article on Marketer-in-Chief. But in short we will now be able to use the marketing tools that we used to buy from the publisher. Now we will have the authority to market the books as we see fit without incurring exorbitant costs.

*T*ips

As a publisher you pay the ISBN, the copyright, and other legal fees.

*E*xample

I promised to discuss CreateSpace and here we go.

When my wife first expressed the desire to start writing novels it fitted right in with the idea of T&R Independent Books. So we immediately began researching what the costs would be to publish.

We searched the internet for both local and online printers. Eventually we settled on CreateSpace because of three primary factors:

1. We would retain ownership of all rights.
2. Costs were reasonable.

3. CreateSpace would provide us worldwide marketing.

These are career changing factors. Although we have and will do our own marketing, being in the CreateSpace loop will expand our marking a thousand times over!

While their imprint will be on our books, there will be no question of who the real publisher is, namely T&R Independent Books.

*A*pplication

In establishing T&R Independent Books we also took over what was formerly known as RFrederickRiddle's Bookstore. It has been renamed T&R Independent Bookstore and markets only books by myself or my wife (under the name Tress Riddle).

Becoming your own publisher is a rather new idea, not original with us. But it has the potential to change the publishing landscape in years to come. You should seriously consider this avenue.

Return to Top

Marketer-in-Chief

Principle

When I wrote my first novel, I knew absolutely nothing about marketing. That doesn't mean I didn't have opinions, but most of those opinions are long gone. Except one!

I realized right up front that most of the marketing would be done by me! I knew that because the publisher told me, but so did common sense. Still, I knew nothing.

After years of trying this and that, I have come to certain conclusions. Marketing:

- is a learning experience
- is knowing there are many experienced writers willing to share their knowledge
- there is much "free" information out there, but be careful
- advertising using traditional methods, such as newspapers and flyers
- advertising using radio and television
- is speaking
- is blogging

- o is newsletters
- o is book signings
- o is discount pricing

These are but ten things that marketing involves, but there are more.

The fact is that as soon as you began writing and before you ever published you became the marketer-in-chief. This is true whether you do it yourself or hire someone. In the end you are responsible.

As Marketer-in-Chief you are responsible for overseeing every aspect of marketing whether you do it or hire someone.

There are professionals who will develop and maintain your website at a price. I did a search on the internet for 'website design' and immediate found seven local designers on the first page. So that is something worth considering.

*T*ips

Most authors don't want to do marketing, but *if you want to succeed then you will find a way.*

As Marketer-in-Chief *you are responsible for overseeing every aspect of marketing whether you do it or hire someone.*

There are professionals **who will develop and maintain websites at a price.**

There are also professionals **who will handle all your marketing needs.**

*E*xample

Over the years my website has change, as it should. It should change frequently. But one area of change is more dramatic.

Originally my home page was boring. It was a little more than an introduction. Then I began learning about content, which is information intelligently placed to inform people about my books. I even placed pictures of my books with calls to action.

But then I began learning and applying advanced marketing techniques. Today my website's home page has less quantity of information, but more valuable content.

This is seen in that the portion above the fold (visible when first appears on screen) is larger than life. In this section is a current promotion. Periodically the offer will change.

Below the fold you will find a pictorial representation of my books and calls to action (buy). This portion of the page will change over time as new books, such as this one, come on line.

The website pages are only one aspect of marketing, but it can require a great deal of time if you do it yourself (as I do). You might consider hiring someone to set up your site and even maintain it for you.

*A*pplication

The first step in marketing is learning. You can't market your products effectively until you know how to market them.

Marketing techniques use the website, social media, newspapers, radio, television, and more. There is an awful lot that needs to be done. It can be daunting to do it yourself. So unless you are wired that way I suggest you hire a professional.

Return to Top

Standard Marketing - (Traditional)

*P*rinciple

Before the internet book marketing was well defined. It was primarily the domain of brick and mortar bookstores. I call this traditional marketing.

Not only was it well defined but it was dominated by the publishing industry. In fact, if you go back far enough the printers of books were also the sellers. Go back still further to the time of Jeremiah and the author was the writer, printer (his scribe Baruch), and distributor.

Just prior to the internet's involvement marketing was dominated by publishers and bookstores. Actually when I first published the internet was here to stay, but the bookstores still dominated.

The story of Borders is classic. This bookstore chain existed for 40 years. When I started writing it was the 2nd largest bookstore chain in American. But only eight years later it folded.

While bookstores are still a huge marketer they are struggling against a powerhouse presence of internet bookstores.

At the time of this writing brick and mortar bookstores are still a viable marketer of books. Many of these bookstores have adjusted and become more flexible enabling them to compete. For authors this means that if you want to do Book Signings you still can, although I have noticed that some no longer do so.

Another traditional marketer is the local library along with regional and national libraries. Unlike bookstores, libraries are not really selling as much as they are buyers. As an author getting your book in the local or not so local library can be significant.

*T*ips

Brick & Mortar Bookstores are still valid outlets for selling your books.

Libraries are excellent places to get your book noticed.

*E*xample

Where I live we now have only two bookstores. One is a Christian bookstore that opened its doors within the past two years. The other is a large chain. Plus we have an extensive library system.

*A*pplication

While bookstores have been hit hard by the internet, they are not necessarily on the way out. In fact, I talked to one store owner who was confident that he could compete successfully against any internet bookseller.

As an author it is good that while it is more difficult to get your books into bookstores and to line up book signings, it can still be done. If that is what you want to do, then don't give up.

Return to Top

Social Marketing

Principle

Social Marketing seems to be constantly changing. This is because social media itself is always changing.

But one unchanging fact stands out: You cannot ignore social media when planning your marketing efforts. Look at this list of social media:

- Bublish
- FaceBook
- GoodReads
- LinkedIn
- Twitter

I call these the big five. You may have others in mind. The thing to remember is that each has something to offer, requires money, has a learning curve, and works.

Probably the most advantageous is FaceBook. With their recent changes they are no longer the robust social outlet (daily posting of what you are doing, etc.). But as a marketing tool they appear unbeatable. Chances are you heard about this book through a Facebook Ad.

When I first learned about social media I signed up for a number of them. I didn't use ads, just the posting abilities. The upshot was that I spent a lot of time socializing and *not creating sales.*

Soon I smartened up and began signing up for training. I also have narrowed my social platform. While all five medias above are still part of my overall platform, I focus my ad campaign on FaceBook.

Everyone of these has marketing tools. Additionally they all tend to relate to FaceBook and Twitter.

As previously indicated all of these have a learning curve. It is not the purpose of this book to provide training in any of these medias. But I do recommend that you sign up for at least two, but no more than five (unless your a glutton for work).

*T*ips

The big 5 social medias are: Bublish, FaceBook, GoodReads, LinkedIn, and Twitter.

Sign up for two or more (no more than 5) and take their training.

*E*xample

When I decided to use FaceBook advertising, I began with Mark Dawson. I also made use of training by Digital Marketer. (By the way, awareness and opportunity for both of these sources came by way of a FaceBook Ad.)

I ended up with Digital Marketer because I couldn't get into Mark's advanced course. But having experienced his initial free course, I am confident that his paid courses are excellent.

But I decided to take the Digital Marketer offer and soon was learning, at my own pace, a great deal of the how-to of FaceBook Advertising. Very thorough with lots of free downloads to help.

Chances are that you learned about this book through a FaceBook ad or my website's home page, both of which are results of my Digital Marketer training.

*A*pplication

Although I have emphasized FaceBook marketing, don't forget the others. Check them out. I for one have been trying to correlate Twitter with FaceBook. Only time will tell how well that works, but I believe it is worthwhile.

You might also explore GoodReads further. Not only can you blog, you can advertise your own books, and even sell from their platform. Bublish is also an excellent choice.

My advice is to connect with all five, then decide which one will be your primary marketing arm. But don't quit the others. If possible, maintain your account with them, interact as much as possible, and use them to compliment and enhance your experience with your primary.

Return to Top

Indie Marketing

Principle

This is called Indie Marketing because it is about the Independent marketer. Which is exactly what you are!

In a sense all your marketing is independent because you have ultimate control. You are an independent businessperson personally managing the marketing of your books. Which is what I am talking about here.

Whether you are marketing traditionally or making use of all the internet tools, you need to be personally involved! But even more so as an independent. This will require your attention to all the details.

Some of this involvement will include scheduling your time. This can be a simple calendar or something more elaborate. I use a daily calendar to plan my activities plus a spreadsheet with greater detail.

You will also need to budget your funds. It is all to easy to spend a few dollars here and a few dollars there. Pretty soon you have a lot of dollars going out!

You can look at each item and justify the expense. But you need to reign it in. Although some offers are extremely inviting (and potentially needed) you need to keep your overall budget in mind.

Marketing aids come in many sizes and shapes. Take a breath and ask yourself if you really need it and can you afford the expense.

*T*ips

Whether you are marketing traditionally or making use of all the internet tools, **you need to be personally involved!**

Use a daily calendar to plan your activities plus a spreadsheet with greater detail.

*E*xample

For our publishing business I make use of our bank's financial tools, which includes budgeting and categorizing. This enables me to track income and expenses in simple, easy to understand manner.

I have designed a budget using a table placed in my word processor. With this I can both track past income/expense and future income/expense.

Indie Marketing is serious business. There's no one else to blame if you mess up. But it's worth it. To be honest, our business at the time of writing this book is still in the beginning stages. That said, we have tools in place for a very successful business.

Application

Still haven't decided to be your own top marketer? Think of it this way: as an author you do the bulk of the work whether writing, publishing or marketing. The writing aspect is obvious, but publishing also requires oversight even if you use a publisher.

And in marketing, you are the top marketer whether you choose to be or not. The difference is the bottom line - the amount of income.

Return to Top

Marketing Aids

*P*rinciple

Only a fool would turn up a nose at marketing aids. You need all the help you can get. The good news is that there are lots of people out there who promise you glorious success, but often they fail to deliver.

I thought it good to provide a list of aids available to you. I don't necessarily vouch for any, but I am listing several aids that I have come across. Check them out and see if they are for you.

A word of caution: When researching tools or services to assist you, do a very thorough job of checking them out. While it is true that I would never list a company that I know is bad, it is possible that over time some have become unreliable. I have done everything I could to eliminate such occurrances.

Here is a list of marketing aids in alphabetical order:
- o Authors Marketing Experts (AME)
- o Aweber
- o Bublish
- o Christian Writers Guild

- Digital Marketer
- FaceBook Ads
- Faithwriters.com
- Godaddy
- MailChimp
- Twitter Ads
- Vertical Response
- Writers Digest

There are many more than these aids, but this should get you started. If nothing else you will certainly learn a great deal.

*T*ips

There are lots of people out there promising you glorious success, **but often they fail to deliver.**

When researching tools or services to assist you, **do a very thorough job of checking them out.**

*E*xample

An example of a service to check out is Authors Marketing Experts (AME). This company founded and operated by Penny Sansevieri is one of the leading book marketers. Not only does she offer programs to market your book she will also take a look at your website and give you a one-time free evaluation. (I have no connection with this service other than I have used it.)

*A*pplication

Marketing Aids are essential to your success as an author. Many authors have used at least some of the aids listed and now their names are well known.

Whatever aids you choose to use follow their ideas and suggestions. None of these guarantee your success but they should give you a leg up.

Sometimes an aid doesn't work out for you. Don't give up. First, evaluate what the aid accomplished. Did you follow directions?

If you did everything right, then maybe that aid is not for you. Find another - there are always others.

Return to Top

Miscellaneous

Principle

This book has provided you with a wide and deep resource on writing, publishing, and marketing. But there is still more.

Don't be afraid of failure. Maybe you've tried over and over to sell your books and nothing happened. Instead of quitting, reexamine everything (including the book itself) and see where you can improve.

While not addressed in this book previously, I suggest you take breaks from your writing. The very act of writing appears to be intensely addictive. Before you know it you are exhausted. **Take breaks**.

Be optimistic. When I first started marketing my own books I wasn't very optimistic about the process at all. Whether it involved approaching a book store about carrying my books or doing a book signing it was scary. *What if I fail*? The answer is persevere, no matter what.

Don't think you have all the answers! Doing so robs you of valuable assistance. There are people out there who may not even be authors that can give valuable advice. Listen! It won't hurt you and it might be just what you need.

If you are a Christian (by this I mean you have received Christ as your Savior) then here's one more piece of valuable information: **Keep in contact with God! Pray regularly**, seeking His Will for you and your writing career. It is an absolute must in a world that is absent of absolutes..

*T*ips

1. Don't be *afraid of failure*.
2. Take *breaks* from your writing.
3. **Don't think you have all the answers!**

If you are a Christian (by this I mean you have received Christ as your Savior) pray regularly, seeking His Will for you and your writing career. It is an absolute must.

*E*xample

One of the reasons I never show my finances, not even book sales, is because seeing others do this has always created a sour taste in my mouth. Often we are shown fabulous profits which tend to set an expectation that almost assures failure.

Your real expectation should not depend on a given amount of money. Rather, you should expect multiplication. In other words, whatever your books are doing now should be increased when you practice the things taught in this book.

And there is another, perhaps more important example of success: What you have learned and what you have done with it.

With that in mind this final application takes a look back at where I started.

I started writing my first book in 2000 and got it published in 2003. As mentioned before I knew next to nothing about book marketing. I had assumed that the publisher would do it.

But even before the book was published, before it was finished, I began learning the value of knowledge. Money is sometimes overrated, whereas knowledge is always necessary.

In looking for a publisher I came face to face with the realities of writing. I was going to need an agent if I went with traditional publishers and would have to do my own negotiating if I went with self-publishers.

By now you know I decided to go with self-publishers. As a new author I had very little say in the contract I signed or in how the book was to be processed. But over the intervening years I have devoted myself to learning more about the publishing and marketing end of authorship. It has been a long hard road, but now I sit with a promising future ahead.

Why?

By taking courses, talking to knowledgeable people, and experimentation I have learned book signing, writing skills, website design, social marketing, and more. I could never have written this book without first gaining the necessary knowledge and skills.

*A*pplication

This book has given you knowledge I did not have when I first started out. What are you going to do with it?

If you are wise you will use this book as a launching pad. Yes, it is designed to give you a good start. But don't stop there. Keep digging, learning, and doing.

Review this book and the Authors Comprehensive Guide (includes Authors Writing Guide, Authors Publishing Guide, and Authors Marketing Guide). Then add to them. Become your own expert!

Then you can start counting the dollars.

Return to Top

ABOUT THE AUTHOR

R. Frederick Riddle is the co-owner of T&R Independent Books. He has authored eleven other books, including the World That Was series.

He is a born again believer who loves the Scriptures and is active in the church.

In 2016 he and his wife launched Author Academy which takes you further and deeper than this book. Simply go to Author Academy and learn how you can benefit. On the following page you have some detail and the offer of a FREE mini-course on not only writing, but publishing and marketing.

Mr. Riddle lives with his wife in Port Charlotte, Florida. Enjoying life as a full-time writer he intends to continue writing for as long as possible.

FREE MINI-COURSE
ON THE
BUSINESS OF WRITING

Just a click away from getting a FREE mini-course on the business of writing. Here you will learn the:

1. Why you're a businessperson?
2. The concept of an Indi business.
3. How to setup your business.

ALL for free, just click here.

T&R INDEPENDENT BOOKS

T&R Independent Books is the owner of T&R Independent Bookstore and the proud publisher of books like the *Did You Know?* series.

At T&R Independent Bookstore you can find:

Did You Know?

      Did You Know American History?

      Did You Know Bible History?

      Did You Know The World That Was?

      Did You Know 2016 Election?

So You Want To Write

The World That Was

      Perished: The World That Was

      The Rise of Shem

      Abraham Called the Friend of God   (coming soon)

Watch for Tress Riddle's debut novel.